No Lunch!

Written by Alison Hawes
Illustrated by Jess Mikhail

Sid and Nan go to the fish
and chip shop to get lunch.

Pad and Pong go with them.

Sid and Nan get chicken
and chips.

Pong wishes she has
chicken to munch.

She jumps up at Sid and Nan.

Pong dashes ... and
dashes ... in rings ...

... and trips up Sid and Nan!

In a flash, Pong is tucking into the lunch.

Sid is cross. Nan is cross.

Pong gets a ticking off
from Sid!

Nan chucks the boxes, but she drops the cash.

Then Sid and Nan rush back
to the fish and chip shop ...

... but Nan has lost the cash!

Pong gets it!